D1825534

PLANNING FOR THE EARLY YEARS

Series editor Jennie Lindon

Food and cooking

How to plan learning opportunities that **engage** and **interest** children

By Jenny Barber

BIRTH TO FIVE

Contents

Published by Practical Pre-School Books, A Division of MA Education Ltd, St Jude's Church, Dulwich Road, Herne Hill, London, SE24 0PB.

Tel: 020 7738 5454   www.practicalpreschoolbooks.com

© MA Education Ltd 2012

Series design: Alison Cutler fonthillcreative 01722 717043

Series editor: Jennie Lindon

All images © MA Education Ltd, other than the images listed below. All photos other than the below taken by Lucie Carlier. Front cover image © iStockphoto.com/David Sucsy.

All rights reserved. No part of this publication may be reproduced, stored in a retrieval system, or transmitted by any means, electronic, mechanical, photocopied or otherwise, without the prior permission of the publisher.

ISBN 978-1-907241-28-4

Author's acknowledgements:

A very big thank you to the staff and children at Acorn Nursery in Shenley Church End, Milton Keynes, who were so welcoming and enthusiastic when I visited to do activities. They are an outstanding nursery in every sense and it was great fun. Thanks also to Mary Jefferson Cobb, childminder in Akeley, Buckinghamshire, who was very supportive of this project, and her minded children, who were fantastic when I visited. I'd also like to say thank you to the lovely group of practitioners I met in Rutland, who embraced the concept of deconstructed cooking in early years and were so admiring of the fruit loaf. Lastly, I have always had a secret dream to write a cookery book and that dream has now partially been fulfilled!

Planning to make a difference for children

A child-friendly approach to planning

Young children benefit from reflective adults who plan ahead on the basis of knowing those children: their current interests and abilities, but also what they are keen to puzzle out and learn. Each title in this series of 'Planning for the Early Years' offers a specific focus for children's learning, with activities for you to fine-tune for young girls and boys whom you know well. These adult-initiated activities happen within a day or session when children have plenty of time for initiating and organising their own play. Your focus for the activities is short term; plan ahead just enough so that everything is poised to go.

Thoughtful planning ensures that children enjoy a variety of interesting experiences that will stretch their physical skills, social and communicative abilities, and their knowledge of their own world. Plans that make a difference for young children connect closely with their current ability and understanding, yet offer a comfortable stretch beyond what is currently easy.

Adult-initiated activities build on children's current interests. However, they are also planned because familiar adults have good reasons to expect that this experience will engage the children. Young children cannot ask to do something again, or develop their own version, until they have that first-time experience. The best plans are flexible; there is scope for the children to influence the details and adults can respond to what actually happens.

Planning is a process that involves thinking, discussing, doing and reflecting. Young children become part of this process, showing you their interests and preferences by their actions just as much as their words, when spoken language develops. Adult planning energy will have created an accessible, well-resourced learning environment – indoors and outdoors. The suggested activities in this book happen against that backdrop and children's new interests can be met by enhancements to the environment – changes that they can help to organise.

Why explore food and cooking with young children

Food and cooking provide a variety of opportunities and experiences for children to explore the properties of food for investigation from a scientific perspective, as well as a chance to introduce the idea of the need to eat and the importance of healthy eating. This will also help children to understand the origins of food, that it doesn't just come from the supermarket, a fact that can be supported with the idea of 'growing your own' in the setting garden or with visits to a pick your own farm or local allotment. Perhaps some of the children grow vegetables or have hens at home.

This book focuses on all the areas of learning and development in the EYFS. Children are making discoveries with something that is familiar to them and they have all experienced. The smell, colour, texture, appearance and feel of the ingredients provide a great sensory stimulus, which should be accentuated and encouraged.

As children make discoveries, both creatively and scientifically, they may be working alone or in a group, thus encouraging both independence and socialisation. There is a great curiosity factor for children as they witness change happening before their eyes, as ingredients combine and consistency and appearance changes, whether this is with play dough or fairy cakes. Through the sensory exploration, language and conversation are stimulated. Through the encouragement of following simple recipes, mathematical understanding is supported thinking about quantity, counting and measuring.

The use of utensils, whether that be their own hands or kitchen tools, stimulates fine motor and manipulative skills, alongside co-ordination and use of the arms and shoulders, particularly for kneading bread or play dough. Understanding of self care and hygiene are also part of the learning process, together with washing hands, keeping your hands on the table and wearing an apron.

Thoughtful adults: effective planning

The adults need to be adventurous and enthusiastic themselves, as well as being prepared to have a go and experiment. Practitioners don't need to be expert cooks themselves or worry that they need particular skills, if not just the desire to go for it. They need to view it as a learning opportunity in conjunction with the children, but it is a good idea to try any of these recipes yourself first if you haven't made anything similar before. Leaders in settings need to consider how to encourage all practitioners to participate and boost confidence. In particular in relation to making play dough with the children and actual cooking activities. Remember to feed off the children's ideas and interests and if something doesn't quite work or is a disaster it doesn't matter! It can still be an enjoyable learning process to explore with the children and have fun. However, some children may be frustrated if their cooking doesn't 'work' for whatever reason, so be ready to acknowledge that as well.

Let the children take the lead and be open to their suggestions and see what unfolds. Use simple recipes measuring in cups, e.g. fruit loaf, or where no real measuring is required just accuracy, e.g. drinks factory. Think about using balancing scales as this adds to the learning experience, bringing in questioning and a careful scrutiny of the scales and use, and understanding of the idea of balance. Either use ones with weights or balancing cups where you are using the weight of eggs to determine the weights of other ingredients being used.

Although these may be planned adult-led activities they still need to allow for flexibility and input from the children. Don't over plan and be prepared for the unexpected. Whilst children may not be able to plan or organise the activities in this book themselves, they can be directly involved in some of the preparation.

It is also worth considering, in terms of cooking activities, what equipment it would be useful to have in the setting. The following is a list of useful utensils: measuring jug, rolling pin, mixing bowls, wooden spoons, weighing scales, pastry cutters, pastry board, chopping board, measuring spoons, whisk, spatula and a collection of knives which would be used under close adult supervision. Tools need to be right for little hands to use but should be proper tools, not play/plastic versions.

Before undertaking any of these activities, it is important to ensure that children wash their hands thoroughly, and that they wear aprons which are specific for cooking, i.e. not painting overalls.

Make sure that your risk assessment relates specifically to the activity being undertaken – who will take things in and out of the oven, where will you put food to cool, do you have a safe place to put the food blender when it is not being used.

The number of children you have in a group will depend on the activity and the children's age. Babies and under-twos should have one adult per two children, whereas for those aged 3-5 probably no more than four children per adult would be a maximum number. If children have enjoyed a breadth of cooking experiences with you, then four- and five-year-olds may cope well within a group of six children to an adult.

The developmental learning journey

The developmental learning journey from birth to five years is broad and long, beginning with the youngest babies, who are exploring the tactile sensations as their senses are stimulated. The stimulation through the fingers triggers the brain, and although babies may have limited physical skills compared with older children, their brains are still as active. As they engage with the experiences they are making discoveries through their senses, handling food stuff, feeling the weight, density and texture.

As they get older, babies and toddlers are keen to extend their skills and explore what they can do with food stuff on offer. Repetition plays an important part in helping them to firm up connections in the brain. This could be a repeated activity or adding to an activity or experience. There is a progression through experience of their understanding of the processes and skills involved in cooking. With babies and the youngest children you might begin by just introducing jelly play by itself and then later add a bowl of warm water or a sprinkling of jelly crystals or corn flour.

Once the basic concepts have been discovered and the experience enjoyed, older children need to be offered extensions to further stimulate and extend learning. They can use pictorial recipe cards to make something for themselves, e.g. play dough. If the recipe cards, ingredients and measuring cups are available to them they could make the dough themselves, with perhaps no or minimal adult input.

They could also be given opportunities to explore with a variety of kitchen tools and utensils, e.g. an electric hand whisk on a low setting, a milk frother and a hand blender. Obviously this would need to be done with careful adult supervision, but it would certainly be a fascinating experience for them to see the effect of the tool or utensil on the food and the consequences of this action, the change of state.

The personal learning journey

The starting point can be based on what the child already knows or has experienced or maybe following an expressed or observed interest. Consider a baby absorbed in flour play, what are they doing submerging their hands, spreading the flour around or patting it down. 'Where might that lead you?' 'What next?' 'What additional resources could you add to the flour?' Glitter, water or maybe rice, how will that develop and extend the experience? Maybe they could experience the flour with their feet instead of their hands.

An older child can offer a myriad of ideas for additional ingredients for play dough, can you support those ideas? Maybe you could look at cookery books featuring different breads and move on to make bread with the children, discussing what they would look or taste like. Encourage the thought processes associated with 'What would happen if...' – children need to be encouraged to be inquisitive. As the children become more skilled and experienced with cooking, you could try out a few alternative ideas to extend their learning, e.g. courgette cake.

Observe and listen carefully to the children's ideas, responses and interests. It makes planning so much easier, as you know you will be providing something that captures their interest and imagination. Children learn much more when learning is in a meaningful context for them and relevant to their interests.

Sometimes story books can provide a stimulus for activity ideas. *The Giant Jam Sandwich* by John Vernon Lloyd is a good example, which gives many points for discussion and thoughts about large scale cookery.

Children make a difference to adult plans

Be flexible, support and allow the children to make a difference to your plans. The plans are for them and not for you, so let them take the lead. Try not to decide everything before an activity begins. If you divert away from the plan it doesn't matter, unless you are following a recipe for a cake. If so, discuss why you need to follow the recipe and what might happen if you don't, or you miss out an ingredient. Could you make two lots, one following the recipe and one following the children's ideas, to be able to compare and contrast the results?

Ensure children can do as much as possible themselves, it is better for each child to have a small bowl each and weigh out their own ingredients instead of everyone sharing a large bowl and taking turns. Children learn best from first hand experiences and they need to be as engaged and involved as possible, which is why individual bowls are better.

If a child says "Can we make the play dough on the floor?" why not make the play dough on the floor in a safe place on plastic sheeting. Or "Can we leave those cakes in the oven a bit longer to see what happens?" maybe leave them for 5 or 10 more minutes to show the difference. Who knows where their ideas and thoughts might lead?

Let go of any pre-conceived ideas you may have in terms of the outcome for an activity, encourage the children to design their own shape for a bread roll – it doesn't have to be round. Resist the temptation to direct the children – let them discover how unworkable sticky dough can be, encourage them to articulate a solution. You may have planned to put paint or icing into icing bags for an activity, but will water or sand work in there? Children need to be able to follow their thoughts and ideas to make connections and discoveries which may lead somewhere else.

Your knowledge of the children extends to knowledge of any allergies they may have and ensuring that you are aware of these in all activities. Remember that, as well as being allergic to food which is eaten, severe allergies may be triggered by merely touching certain foods.

Experiences worth talking and thinking about

Remember silence is important for thinking. Children need the space to think and make connections and reflect on what they have seen or are doing. Let the children take the lead with conversation. Make thought-provoking statements and ask open-ended questions:

"The cakes smell delicious while cooking in the oven."

"I wonder what would happen if we used a bigger cup for measuring?"

"Will it still work if we put holes in the icing bag?"

"What will happen if we don't weigh and measure the ingredients properly?"

The activities need to be positive communication experiences for the children. As they play they are making discoveries upon which they will need to reflect. We need to view the activities as a voyage of discovery for us in terms of what we can learn about the children, and this includes their verbal and non-verbal communications. By observing and listening we will gain that knowledge.

With babies and the youngest children, mimic their verbal utterances and engage in parallel talk. This should describe what they are doing – not as a running commentary but intermittently; be sensitive and listen. Describe the sensory experience from your perspective to develop language and vocabulary.

With many of the activities for the older children there are a wealth of opportunities to introduce new vocabulary, descriptive words describing sensations and reactions and discussion as to how ingredients are working and combining together. Take the opportunity to use in context and explain culinary terms, as described in some of the activities in this book. We must at all times, though, remember the importance of sitting back observing and listening, to avoid the danger of perpetual direction, of conversation and chat.

Looking at cookery books and books about food as a supporting resource can stimulate chat and thoughts and potentially generate ideas as to what the children might like to create or have a go at making.

Scope for creativity

In some respects the scope for creativity can be limited with cooking activities, as often a recipe needs to be followed, but there are opportunities for children to be creative in terms of how they decorate a cake or shape a bread roll. Options for creativity present themselves with play dough – trying out different additional ingredients, finding out how that changes the feel and density of the dough or 'does it work?' If children are engaging with the experimental cookery activity where they can mix and choose from a selection of differing ingredients, creativity is encouraged as they make discoveries. The described activity 'experimental cooking' is about allowing children to discover for themselves what happens if you use a variety of ingredients in different ways.

Cookery can allow children some opportunities to experiment and see what happens if they use different ingredients, as ultimately that is how recipes are developed and new ingredient combinations discovered, and potentially where the innovative cooks for tomorrow will come from! It might not happen now in our settings, but it is about what we are building the foundations for in terms of ideas for later in life. If you don't experiment you'll never know. Through exploring food and cooking we can encourage this to happen. Think about the direction in which an activity can go, which reflects creativity, try to go about with different ideas, showing children an imaginative use of the ingredients.

Children may recreate cooking activities in their imaginative play, perhaps using play dough or in experimental cooking, exploring a creative process. What choices and decisions do they make about how they wish to explore jelly? How do they choose to mix the ingredients for fruit loaf? What flavour combinations are chosen in the drinks factory?

UK Frameworks and planning

Early childhood starts with babies and stretches to five or six years of age. Within the four nations of the UK, England is the only country to have moved to a Birth to Five years framework. Northern Ireland, Scotland and Wales all have two documents to cover the early years span. (See page 32 for references.) However, similar principles within national documents emphasise that:

- Practitioners need to take a personalised approach, supported by flexible planning that takes full account of the current abilities of individual babies and children, as well as likely next steps.

- Young children learn best when there is plenty of scope for child-initiated activities, within a learning environment well resourced for play and friendly conversation.

- Adult-initiated activities should enable children to be mentally and physically active within those experiences and children's interests influence the development of adult plans.

- Headings for aspects of development vary, but the consistent message is that child development is holistic. The areas of learning are presented separately to ensure that nothing is overlooked. Yet, day-by-day, young children, absorbed in an engaging activity, will learn in ways that combine several different areas.

Children's secure learning depends on practitioners who value, nurture and foster close relationships with children and their family.

Early years practitioners need to be very familiar with their relevant national framework, including the way in which areas of development are organised. Different phrases are used to refer to aspects of children's learning. Yet, there is a consistent emphasis on the central importance of young children's personal, social and emotional development and on building a secure base of communication and spoken language. Along with active respect for children's physical development and wellbeing, these areas of development are the crucial foundations for other areas of young learning.

Wherever early years practitioners live and work, they need to grasp how young children make sense of the early mathematical concepts and how they extend their general knowledge of the wider world. A flair for creative expression should be nurtured in early childhood and the national frameworks acknowledge that creativity is as much about how children think as the pleasure in making something tangible.

The approach to planning, in each national framework, links the key components of:

- **Alert observation** by practitioners who come to know individual children very well. Observation is a combination of spontaneously noticing what children do and a more planned watching and listening.

- **Assessment** – a process of making sense – of what has been observed, so that understanding can inform what is offered to individual children and small groups in the immediate and relatively near future.

- **Short-term planning** shown in adult actions to add resources, so that children can extend their observed interests. Equally short-term, flexible planning for adult-initiated (and maybe adult-led) activities that are likely to engage children and stretch their current abilities or knowledge.

This continual approach is sometimes described as a 'planning cycle', because it is ongoing. Observation, assessment and planning are not separate practitioner activities, each in their own little box. Adult thoughtfulness can be provoked at any point: by what you observe, what you have learned by bringing together your knowledge of this child, and by events within spontaneous play and conversation, or slightly more organised activities. Finally, national early years frameworks raise the importance of children being involved in the process of planning, appropriately for their age. Young children need to be confident that their views and preferences, however expressed, make a difference to what happens day by day.

Making connections with home life

Find out what food children enjoy eating at home. Who does the cooking at home? Do they help with the cooking? Perhaps a photo board could be created of the children cooking at home.

Do you have any parents who are skilled cooks, maybe it is their profession or perhaps something they enjoy or take pleasure from? Can they come in to the setting to share something with the children? Or could parents come in and share foods from their culture with the children? Maybe you could organise a special 'food around the world' day. Parents might not want to come in and cook with the children, but they may have ideas of what could be cooked in the setting.

Many families have family favourites or recipes that have been passed through generations, or particular meals or food they have on certain days of the week or during particular celebrations. When I was a child we always had boiled egg for breakfast on a Sunday, that was a family tradition. It can be something as simple as that, not necessarily an elaborate meal!

Children could take the gingerbread biscuit recipe home with them, so they could make them at home. Perhaps they could bring in to the setting a particular strong-smelling herb or spice, which could be smelled by other children, used and talked about in an activity. If you don't have herbs in the garden of your setting, perhaps one of your parents could bring in selection of herbs from their garden.

Alternatively, you could simply ask the parents how they feel about being involved and in what way – you never know what suggestions and ideas they might have to share.

Learning about jelly

Jelly is a fantastic resource to use with children as it is readily available and accessible to all. It offers many options and can be presented as a solid or a liquid. Some practitioners might be reluctant for children to play with 'food', as they feel that food should be eaten not 'wasted', so it is important to be aware of the learning opportunities for the children.

Jelly can be experienced by children in a variety of ways depending on their age and stage of development, for example on the tray of a highchair or in a tuff spot on the floor.

Initially children can engage and explore with just their hands, enjoying the tactile experience. This is particularly important for the youngest babies, relishing the sensory stimulation. Older children may wish to use tools, especially if other substances are being added to the jelly.

You might choose to present set jelly or jelly cubes to the children, or perhaps both, with a bowl of warm water by the side for the children to use in their experiments. Maybe add both the set jelly and jelly cubes to the warm water for them to see the effect. Colour variations are another option, as is sprinkling in jelly crystals or perhaps the addition of ice cubes or corn flour.

It is essential that children can explore, discover and experiment with the jelly simply for the substance that it is, without being directed or hindered with the addition of animals or cars into the jelly. It can be tempting to add resources thinking it will make the experience more interesting for the children, but this is unnecessary as the children need to explore and experience the jelly for itself.

An opportunity to learn about jelly

Playing with jelly provides stimulation and exercise for the muscles in the fingers, hands and forearms, while supporting manipulative skills and hand and eye coordination. Young children can discover ways to move and transport the jelly, perhaps experiment watching it slide down a slope or squelch and squish in their hands. Can children use their hands to transport set jelly or do they need a tool? How does the transportation of set jelly differ from that of jelly cubes?

Encourage the children to experiment: what happens to jelly cubes put in cold water and jelly cubes put in warm water? If you put jelly cubes, ice cubes and sugar cubes on a tray, what happens to them? This exercise can encourage prediction and produces a surprising result for the children. What happens if you put jelly in the water tray – does it float, sink or dissolve?

What do you need to do beforehand?

- If you are using hot water, think about how this will be transported to the table, how you can make the children aware of the danger. Consider the floor and what to do if there were any spillages.
- Decide where and how the experience will be presented to the children. Will it be a messy play experience or are you going to include the scientific aspect as well?
- Will it be an individual or group activity?
- If you are presenting set jelly to the children ensure the jelly has had time to set.
- Will it be a child-initiated or adult-led experience?
- Is the jelly activity made available for the children to access as they wish throughout the session without any adult input? If they wish could the children move the jelly to other areas – perhaps the water tray or the home corner?
- Collect together all the necessary resources: jelly cubes, jelly crystals, bowls, trays, jug of cold water, hot water, spoons, aprons.

Babies and younger children begin with an initial visual stimulus, then, as they touch and smell, they are making connections between what their eyes tell them and what their hands feel.

If children are involved in dissolving the jelly cubes and waiting for the jelly to re-set, they are experiencing first hand the change of state of the jelly, as well as cause and effect as the water reacts with the jelly cubes. They can see and feel the similarities and differences between the two solid states of the set jelly and jelly cubes, the texture, density and colour.

Responding to children's and babies' interests

You need to observe and listen to the children to see what is interesting and stimulating to them. How do they react? Verbal utterances or words and facial expression? Do they seek out additional resources themselves? Do they attempt to pile up the jelly into a mound or flatten it out or attempt to make shapes or other constructions with the jelly?

Can the jelly be set in moulds? What could the children find in the setting to use as moulds?

Could the children cut the jelly with scissors? Is there a difference between attempting to cut the set jelly and the jelly cubes? Can they push the jelly through a sieve or mash it using a potato masher?

Put objects in the jelly before it is set, to be uncovered and discovered. Present it to the children on the floor on an old shower curtain, sprinkled with glitter or corn flour.

Time for you to think

How did the children engage with the activity? Were they able to follow through on ideas, could the jelly be extended into other areas of exploration? Was it the sensory and textural experience they enjoyed most or did they prefer experimenting and finding out? Were they most interested in cutting the jelly or push it through a sieve/potato masher? Did that vary for different children? Could you introduce more dissolving and melting experiences, to follow on with experiencing change of state of different substances? Were children making surprising links and connections? What comments did they make about their discoveries? What does this tell you about their understanding and what can you do with this knowledge?

Listening to children and talking with them

With babies and the younger children you could engage in parallel talk, introducing words to describe their actions. With this kind of play the words can beautifully sum up the sound and feel of the jelly on hands, e.g. squidgy, squelchy, squeezy.

Using supportive, thought-provoking statements is an effective way to encourage older children. "The jelly is making a noise as you squeeze it" "It's cold, it's slimy, it's disappearing". You don't want to be intrusive, distracting the thought processes occurring in the children's brains as they play. Remember, sometimes, it is better to say nothing.

Use questions that could lead to discussion, prediction or generate ideas: "How can we get the jelly out of the mould?" "I wonder how we can make a stripy jelly of different colours" "Do you think we could pile the jelly up in a tower?"

If children enjoy having their hands in the jelly, can they clap their hands or hide their hands in it?

Encourage the children to take the lead, discussing their observations and thoughts.

Learning about cheese scones

Cheese scones are quick to make, easy and delicious. They can be made in individual bowls or altogether in one large bowl. The children can shape their scones using their hands, to make them individual. The recipe is very straightforward and can easily be accessed by children of a variety of ages.

The measures listed first are for scones made in groups and the second measure listed is for scones made by the individual child, but the method is the same for both versions. The larger quantity will make around 6 scones, depending on size.

What do you need to do beforehand?

- Collect together the ingredients and if you wish grate the cheese in preparation.
| This could be an opportunity to undertake a shopping trip with the children beforehand. They can help select ingredients from the shelf and also an interesting discussion may ensue about the origin of the ingredients.
- Collect the utensils – mixing bowl, weighing scales, measuring jug, wooden spoon, baking tray.
| Decide if the children will be working together or if they will have their own individual bowls, ensuring you have enough if it is to be individually.
- As you will use an oven, ensure you are the person who takes things in and out of the oven and that you know where the scones will be put to cool.
- Help the children prepare name labels to place by their scones on the baking tray, so that you know whose is whose, after they have been cooked.
- Consider if the children will be eating the scones in the setting or taking them home.
| Think about how many children will be an easily manageable number to work with at one time, usually between four and six.

Recipe for cheese scones

For a group	For individual children
200g self-raising flour	50g self-raising flour
50g soft butter or margarine	12g soft butter or margarine
50g grated cheese	1 dessert spoon of grated cheese
150ml milk	40ml milk

What you need to do:

1. Heat the oven to 200°C or gas mark 6

2. Sift the flour into a bowl and rub the butter or margarine into the flour until it resembles breadcrumbs.

3. Stir in the cheese using a spoon, followed by the milk.

4. Using your hand combine the ingredients together to make a dough, if necessary add more milk or flour to combine.

5. Shape the scone/s using hands or a pastry cutter and place on a greased baking tray, sprinkle extra cheese on top.

6. Bake for 10-15 minutes until golden.

An opportunity to learn about making scones

Through making cheese scones, the children will have an opportunity to learn the technique of 'rubbing in', a useful skill for young cooks to master. Using this method is likely to strengthen the muscles in their fingers and hands and support the development of their manual dexterity. It also adds to the sensory experience as they feel the flour and butter on their fingers, and how the texture changes, as the two combine. This is complimented by the control and hand and eye co-ordination required to use the sieve effectively and the pleasure of seeing the flour drift through the holes of the sieve.

They will experience measuring both solids and liquids, seeing the weight of the flour and butter on the scales and watching the dial move round and the volume of the milk in a measuring jug. As the ingredients mix and combine, they can see the change of state from dry and wet to a solid lump, which they can then mould and shape with their hands or a pastry cutter to make their scone. This is developed further as they see the change in colour and shape after the scones have been cooked. If cheese has been sprinkled on the top they will see how it has melted and turned golden.

Responding to children's and babies' interests

If the children enjoyed the scones you could make them with different added ingredients to change the flavour, e.g. ham (if all the children are able to eat this), or add chives which are easy for children to snip.

You could also make sweet scones by replacing the cheese with 2 heaped tablespoons of caster sugar plus 50g sultanas (scones made together) or a level dessert spoon of caster sugar and half a dessert spoon of sultanas for individual scones. Were the children interested in using the weighing scales? Could you introduce other types of scales for weighing or measuring?

Time for you to think

Were there any children who were reluctant to be involved, or were unsure how to do some of the required techniques, e.g. 'rubbing in'? Do they need to watch others first to help build their confidence, or could they begin by being involved with some aspects, e.g. weighing and mixing before progressing to the rubbing in? If the children were mixing the ingredients together in one large bowl, instead of making individual scones, could they make one large round scone to share? This would then reinforce the idea of working together.

Listening to children and talking with them

Think about the descriptions of techniques and instructions that you can use. Use the tips of your fingers to dance around the butter and flour, and then squeeze them between the fingertips so you have rubbed the flour and butter together. Discuss with them carefully measuring using a spoon, levelling out the surface and then carefully tipping the contents into their bowl. Can they then make the cheese disappear and hide in the flour and butter mixture? Do they need more milk to make their scone shape or have they got too much, what could they add more of if they have too much milk? If you pose a question or make a comment, leave time for the children to reflect and respond.

What shape would they like their scone to be? They could make several mini scones.

Perhaps cheese is a favourite food for some children. Does cheese normally look like this, grated? In what other ways have they seen cheese? Do they like cheese, have they had cheese sandwiches, do they like cheese on toast, do they have squeezy cheese? What do they think will happen to the cheese once it is in the oven?

What other things could we add to the scones instead of cheese?

Do they think they will be able to eat the scones as soon as they come out of the oven? What might stop them from being able to eat them straightaway?

Learning about courgette cake

Most children enjoy eating cakes. While some may never have made cakes, others might, so this recipe is about trying something different and opening up a different idea.

Courgette cake is similar in texture and taste to carrot cake, but simply using a different vegetable. It is an easy cake to make and explores with the children other uses for vegetables, which is expanding their knowledge and their taste. The cake also promotes healthy eating as it is vegetable-based, and low in fat as it uses sunflower oil.

Although the cake needs to be made in one large bowl the children can be involved in all the stages. Extremely careful supervision would be needed if they were to explore grating the courgettes –

What do you need to do beforehand?

- Collect together the ingredients, it is probably best to grate the courgettes in advance, perhaps leaving just one to either grate with the children or in front of the children.
- The children can help to gather all the necessary utensils – weighing scales, measuring jug, wooden spoon, large mixing bowl, grater, balloon whisk, teaspoon and loaf tin.
- Make sure you know who will be using the oven and where the cake will cool.
- Decide when you are going to eat the cake.
- Consider and plan which aspects of the cake making the children will be involved with, ensuring this is as much as possible, from weighing the ingredients to greasing and lining the loaf tin.
- Plan the time to make the cake, allowing for cooking and cooling. You will need to allow about 2 hours for the whole process.

Recipe for courgette cake

4 courgettes – grated, 1 egg, 125ml sunflower oil, 200g self-raising flour, 150g soft brown sugar, 1 teaspoon of cinnamon, ½ teaspoon of nutmeg.

What you need to do:

1. Pre-heat the oven to 170°C or gas mark 3, grease the bottom of the tin by brushing with oil and base line a loaf tin with greaseproof paper, or if available use a paper loaf tin liner.

2. Whisk the egg in a large bowl

3. Mix the courgettes and oil into the bowl with the egg using a wooden spoon.

4. Sieve the flour onto the wet ingredients, add the sugar and spices and mix well.

5. Pour into a greased loaf tin and bake for about an hour and leave the cake to cool in the tin.

the practitioner could hold the grater steady as the child carefully moves the courgette up and down the grater. The child would need to be shown how to hold and place the courgette on the grater and move it up and down.

An opportunity to learn about courgette cake

A key element of this recipe is use of a vegetable in a cake. Introducing the children to the variety of ways in which we can use vegetables may help to change any thoughts they may have about not liking vegetables. Older children can see how the state of the courgette changes as it is grated, and that it is very moist and quite watery.

Often we cook with caster sugar, but this recipe uses soft brown sugar so they can see sugar in a different form, in both grain size and colour. Do they think this will change the taste? They can also smell the two spices, do they like the smell, does it make them think of anything in particular?

Also, often in recipes the wet ingredients are added to the dry, but with this one it is the other way round. It is just about mixing the ingredients, so they can see the change of state and the little green threads of the grated courgette.

Once the cake has been cooked, cooled and sliced, they can see how the colour has changed but they can still see the green courgette and the effect of heat on the ingredients.

Responding to children's and babies' interests

Making a carrot cake could follow on from this recipe – you can also make cakes using parsnips and beetroot (beetroot mixes particularly well with chocolate). The over threes could help you research other recipes.

Looking at the grated courgette how does it differ from the whole courgette, what else can be shredded or grated? If you have made the cheese scones on page 10 you could refer back to them as the cheese is grated.

You can describe to the children how to make an emulsion. When cooking, this means combining two ingredients which would not normally mix together (in this case oil and egg, in particular egg yolk), but by whisking carefully they will mix together.

Did the children like the cake and its taste? Were they interested by the idea of using vegetables in a cake, do they want to do more of the same? Were there other aspects of this recipe that triggered an interest? Did they like smelling the spices and tried to mix them together? Were they able to use prior knowledge and transfer skills from other cooking-related activities when making this cake? How can you build on what has been seen and learnt in this activity? Did they find the idea of oil emulsions interesting, do they want to make more cakes using vegetables, can you research these together and go out and buy the vegetables?

Listening to children and talking with them

You could begin by asking the children what they think the process of making the cake will be and what they will need to do first. Which ingredients do they think they will mix first? Do they know what all the ingredients are and where do they think they come from? What do they think will happen when the ingredients combine? This line of questioning is presuming some prior experience of cooking, but it can be changed. If they have had prior experience you can see what they have remembered.

The children might notice that in this recipe you use sunflower oil. The oil could be experimented with – can you find anything that you can mix with the oil? What happens when you add water to the oil, looking at how the water is suspended in the oil?

You could use further questions to draw out more discussion which may lead the children to ask about different processes and aspects of the recipe. "Why are we adding the spices?" "Which of the spices do they prefer?"

What do the children think would happen if the courgettes weren't grated? Could they have gone in whole or sliced into pieces? Do they think that would work in the cake?

Learning about focaccia bread

Making bread with children is a great cooking activity, they are used to kneading dough from using play dough and the exciting element of bread is that it grows and changes shape. This recipe contains quite a lot of yeast and so rises beautifully, much to the children's pleasure, although it does require a certain amount of patience! Bread is also a very accessible activity for children from two years up as they can all be involved in kneading the dough.

This is best done altogether in one very large bowl. The key aspect is the kneading which everyone can enjoy.

The secret of good bread is in the kneading. To knead you need to get stuck in using your whole hand, moving the dough backwards and forwards using your palms, and pushing it with your fists and knuckles.

An opportunity to learn about making focaccia bread

The key learning opportunity with bread is the effect of the yeast, and how the dough grows and becomes bubbly,

What do you need to do beforehand?

- Collect together the ingredients and utensils. You will need a very large mixing bowl, measuring jug, two tablespoons, a wooden spoon, tea towel or cling film and a large baking tin.
- Work out the timings, including the time to rise (prove). This bread takes quite a while to make – around 3 hours in total.
- Decide where would be the best place to leave the dough to rise, it needs to be in a warm place where it won't matter if it spills out of the bowl.
- Consider which aspects the children can be involved with.

Recipe for focaccia bread

500g plain flour, 500g strong plain bread flour, 25g salt, 500ml warm water, 3 packets of dried yeast, 3 tablespoons of runny honey, 3 tablespoons of olive oil

What you need to do:

1. Sieve the flour and salt into a very large bowl.

2. Make a well in the middle of the flour and add the water, yeast, honey and olive oil.

3. Combine together with a spoon and then take out of the bowl and knead on a floured table top, pushing, pulling and folding. Keep kneading until it feels elastic, which will take about 3-5 minutes.

4. Put the dough back in the bowl, cover the bowl with cling film or a tea towel and leave in a warm place for an hour.

5. Once the dough has risen knock it back (knead it again to knock out the air bubbles). It will reduce in size but that is part of the process. Place the knocked back dough in a greased baking tin, cover and leave to rise again for about half an hour.

6. Once risen bake in a hot oven 220°C or gas mark 7 for about 40 minutes until golden.

light, springy and elastic to feel. The warmth and sugar allow the yeast to ferment which releases carbon dioxide gas – this is what makes the bread rise. It is useful to take photos as the bread rises, so that the children can see and then compare and contrast how it changes. They will need to touch and gently prod the dough at intervals to feel the difference. Children also learn that you don't just buy bread, you can make it as well.

Making any kind of bread is excellent for manipulative skills, such as co-ordination of the arms and muscle control in the upper arm, as the children knead and pound the dough. Encourage the children to stand up for this as they can then exert more pressure and energy into the dough, this should also be done on a floured table top. An adult may need to model the kneading action for the children. If a flour shaker is available they will be able to sprinkle a little on if the dough and their fingers become a little sticky.

Once the bread has been baked children can be shown how to tap the bottom of the bread, to listen for a hollow sound indicating that the bread is cooked.

Responding to children's and babies' interests

The children are very likely to display an interest with the rising bread and therefore the role of the yeast in the process. If you have an extra packet of dried yeast, put it into a jug with 100ml of warm water and a little sugar. The yeast will froth up and produce a yeasty smell, which can help their understanding. You might be able to get hold of some fresh yeast for the children to see and experience in the same way as the dried yeast. You could get this from a supermarket in-store bakery or independent bakers shop.

The bread does not need to be baked as a loaf and the children may, during the knocking back process (second kneading), want to make their own shaped smaller loaves or rolls, particularly if they are encouraged to make a mixture of shapes and sizes as with play dough.

You can extend interest with a visit to a bakery.

Time for you to think

What skills, techniques and understanding did the children demonstrate? Could they see how the yeast made the dough rise? Were they fully aware of and did they understand the processes involved? Were they able to hear the hollow sound of the cooked bread? Did the children particularly like to experiment making different sizes and shapes, to make their own individual loaves or rolls? Did they prefer to make one loaf to share together or their own individual rolls or mini loaves? Were the children able to involve their whole body enthusiastically as they stood to knead the dough? Were there some children who were very tentative with the kneading movement?

Listening to children and talking with them

Use the opportunity to introduce to the children terminology associated with making bread, e.g, kneading the dough, leaving it to prove when it is left to rise and knocking back when you knead it for the second time. Encourage discussion of descriptive words for the feel of the dough: light, spongy, elastic, sticky, bubbly and action words for the kneading of the dough, e.g. thumping, pushing, pummelling, pounding, pressing and squeezing.

Discuss what shapes can be made with the dough, is it easy to manipulate? Think and discuss with the children words to describe the change in the dough as it rises, e.g. increase, gain, burgeon, expand, grow.

Pose thought-provoking questions, but also allow time for the children to respond and ask their own questions. You might ask "What do you think would happen if we added yeast to our play dough?" "What do you think the bread would be like if we didn't add the yeast?" "Why do you think we have to knead the dough?" The children might ask you if the dough could rise and grow so much it reached the ceiling? "What could we do if it rose so much it didn't fit into the oven?" "Could we make bread for a giant?" "How can we squeeze the dough into this loaf tin?"

Learning about fruit loaf

This is a very simple-to-follow recipe which only uses a cup for measuring so is suitable for the under threes as well as older children. Older children would be able to follow a pictorial recipe card and manage the activity for themselves.

It doesn't matter what size cup you use, as long as you use the same cup for each measurement – obviously the larger the cup, the larger the finished loaf will be. Once baked, it makes a great treat for snack time.

You could make one large loaf, or if the children use a cup from a tea set and you have access to mini loaf tins, they could make their own individual fruit loaves.

What do you need to do beforehand?

- Collect together the ingredients and utensils – you will need a mixing bowl, wooden spoon, cup and a loaf tin. You could create a picture checklist so the children can help find what is needed.
- Choose your cup for measuring, a small mug works well, but if you want to make a larger loaf select a larger cup or mug.
- If the children participating in the activity are developmentally able, consider getting them to lead the activity for themselves and prepare a pictorial recipe card for them to use. You and the children can also decide if they are going to make one large loaf or smaller individual loaves.
- If you have the available ingredients, consider letting the children decide on the mixture of dried fruit they wish to use in the loaf, so try to have a range available.
- With this recipe you need to ensure you allow enough time for the hour of soaking and the hour of cooking, plus the preparation time. The cooking time will be reduced if you are making small individual loaves.

Recipe for fruit loaf

1 cup of All Bran, 1 cup of mixed dried fruit (use any combination mixture of currants, sultanas and raisins), ½ cup of demerara sugar, 1 cup of milk, 1 cup of self-raising flour.

What you need to do:

1. Pre-heat the oven to 150°C or gas mark 2.

2. Mix all the ingredients, except the self-raising flour, together in a bowl, then cover and leave to soak for an hour. A ticking kitchen timer could be used, so the children can hear the timer go off.

3. After the ingredients have soaked for an hour, add the cup of self-raising flour and mix.

4. Pour the ingredients into a greased loaf tin and bake for an hour. You can, if you wish, sprinkle extra demerara sugar on the top.

An opportunity to learn about fruit loaf

This recipe provides a great opportunity for using a non-standard unit of measure in a flexible way. There is a choice of the size of the measure itself, but once selected you have to stick with that measure. This can provide discussion as to why this is important and how the outcome of the recipe could be affected. This also leads to refining the skill of filling the cup with each ingredient in turn levelling off the surface of the cup, then manipulating the cup to empty the ingredients into the bowl.

The children can see the All Bran absorbs the milk and changes from being hard and twig-like in appearance to being soft and squidgy. How the ingredients mush

down together and how that changes again as the flour is added before cooking.

Responding to children's and babies' interests

The children could choose which dried fruit to use in the loaf, they could taste sultanas, raisins and currants to aid the decision. Other dried fruits could also be offered, e.g. dried apricots, figs, dates. This might lead to further experiments, like making different versions of the fruit loaf with different mixtures of dried fruits.

You could experiment with soaking All Bran in other liquids to see how it changes, this could simply be cold water and warm water. Consider with the children where the liquid goes and how it disappears, could the liquid state be returned? You could try further experimenting with sponges, cloths, kitchen towel and paper to look at the absorption of water, what does absorb and what doesn't and which is the most effective? If you measure some water, soak it up in a sponge, and once it has been absorbed squeeze out the water and measure it again to see if the volume of water is the same or less. The children could predict what they think the result will be.

There is also a tactile element – the children could explore and contrast the feel of the dry All Bran and the soaked All Bran. What happens if they squeeze the soaked All Bran?

You could also look at different sized cups for measuring, filling, emptying and comparing the quantities each cup holds. These quantities could then be weighed or measured in a measuring jug to see if the difference noted by the eye is the same as the actual measured quantity.

Time for you to think

What were the key interests of the children? Were they able to successfully measure using the cups? What was their understanding of 'capacity' in relation to filling the cup? Next time could the children lead themselves with this cooking activity? Would it be better next time to use a larger or smaller cup for measuring? What surprises were there about the children's knowledge, awareness and understanding? What do you now know that you didn't know before about the children in terms of their skills and understanding? How can that knowledge be used?

Listening to children and talking with them

Ask the children to describe what the All Bran looks like, it can be helpful to get them to trickle it through their fingers first, to get a sense of the feel to aid the description. It is important not to influence the children with descriptive vocabulary initially, but to see what ideas and thoughts they have.

There is much opportunity for use of positional and mathematical vocabulary as you make the fruit loaf. Discuss filling the cup up to the top, then the need to empty the cup into the bowl, by turning the cup over and tipping the cup up. Talk to the children about shaking the cup and tapping the bottom to ensure all the measured ingredients have emptied out. Ask them what they think would be the best way to hold the cup above the bowl to empty out the ingredients.

As they add the ingredients ask, them what they think would happen if we added more than one cup of an ingredient? Encourage them to think about the quantity of the ingredients, considering that, although we have used the same size cup to measure, does it look as if there is more of one ingredient than another?

Before you set the ingredients aside to soak for an hour, encourage the children to predict what they think will happen whilst they are left to soak? Once the hour of soaking is over ask the children what they think has happened to the milk and what else can they see has happened?

Learning about gingerbread biscuits

Many children love cooking, making something of your own which you can eat is exciting. These biscuits can be made into any shape or design. If the children are provided with a variety of cutters they can choose to use a cutter or maybe fashion their own biscuit shapes using their hands. This is an activity for a small group of children as the ingredients need to be made in one large bowl, but they can be involved in all the stages. Children who are over two can enjoy this activity, and as their experience and skills develop they can be more and more involved with the process.

An opportunity to learn about making gingerbread biscuits

Children have an opportunity to develop practical cookery skills and be encouraged to practice weighing and sieving ingredients, combining them, rubbing in and rolling out. They will also need a certain degree of precision and accuracy combined with manual dexterity

What do you need to do beforehand?

- Collect together the necessary ingredients and utensils – one large mixing bowl, one small mixing bowl, weighing scales, biscuit cutters, a tablespoon, 2 teaspoons, wooden spoon for mixing, sieve, small child-sized rolling pins and fork.
- Think about how the biscuits will be taken to and from the oven, considering any safety issues and where they will be cooled.
- Consider whether the children will eat the biscuits in the setting or if they will be taken home. Could the adult involved make another batch that is available for general eating and enjoyment, allowing the children who have been involved in the activity to eat their own biscuits?

Recipe for gingerbread biscuits

350g plain flour, 2 teaspoons ground ginger, 1 teaspoon bicarbonate of soda, 100g soft butter or margarine, cut into cubes, 175g light soft brown sugar, 1 egg, 4 tablespoons of golden syrup (easier to use a squeezy bottle).

What you need to do:

1. Pre-heat the oven to 180°C or gas mark 5.

2. Sift the flour, ginger and bicarbonate of soda into a bowl, stir in the cubes of butter until they are coated in flour.

3. Rub the butter into the flour until it resembles breadcrumbs, then stir in the sugar.

4. In a separate bowl combine the egg and syrup together using a fork and then stir into the flour mixture. Mix together with a spoon until you have made a dough (like that made for the focaccia bread – see page 14) and knead until it is smooth.

5. Dust some flour onto the table surface, the dough could then be divided between the children so they can all roll out the dough and then choose their cutters to create the biscuits.

6. Place the biscuits onto greased baking trays and bake for 12-20 minutes. Once baked, leave them on the baking tray for 5 minutes before moving them to a cooling rack.

to be able to cut out the shapes or mould them, manoeuvre them onto the baking tray and also measure out the teaspoons of ginger and bicarbonate of soda.

If the children have made play dough or the focaccia bread (see page 14) they will be experienced with kneading, but here they are repeating this skill for a different purpose with a different end result, the biscuits are very different to bread, but making them uses the same technique.

They can see the change of state and colour of the ingredients as they combine, and smell the ginger as it is added to the bowl. Once cracked open they can see the contrasting yolk and white of the egg, then how they merge into a yellow liquid as they are combined. Once they have mixed the ingredients, they can consider if it is too dry or too wet. Does something else need to be added to alter the consistency, or is it just right?

Responding to children's and babies' interests

If you have used the icing bags (see page 28) as a mark making activity, it will be great for the children to use them for the appropriate purpose. If given a choice of decorative items and colours of icing, they can make their biscuits very individual, bringing in an element of creativity.

Ginger is the main flavour in these biscuits. You could look at root ginger (available in greengrocers or in the fruit and vegetable section in a supermarket), stem ginger which comes in syrup in a jar, crystallized ginger which is seen as confectionary and ground ginger (in the spice jar). The differences can lead to discussion, as you grate the knobbly root ginger and cut up the stem and crystallized ginger.

Many children will enjoy rolling out the dough. Can you provide rolling out on a larger scale – with play dough using a larger rolling pin, or dough on the floor using a broom handle. Experience rolling with paint using a paint roller.

Time for you to think

Could the activity have been presented differently to the children, are there any additional resources or utensils they would have been useful? Is there more the children could do or was it just right? Which of the cookery skills were they particularly proficient with, how could they be developed? Did you learn anything about hand preference or manipulative skills? Did any of the children struggle to use a rolling pin or to use the cutters? If they did, what experiences could be provided to help them develop their skills?

Listening to children and talking with them

Introduce the correct terminology for each of the cookery skills used, either through self talk if you are engaged or parallel talk as the children engage with the activity, giving an explanation of what each one means; use the terms weighing, measuring, sieving, combining, mixing, kneading, rolling and cutting. Explain that we sieve the flour so that there are no lumps, and to let in air so that the ingredients mix better. Explain that we need to measure and weigh the ingredients so we have the right quantities or amounts to make the biscuits. Encourage them to think about what would happen if we added too much or too little of one ingredient.

As you add the different ingredients ask the children thought-provoking questions and make statements to affirm and stimulate thought. "Are all the ingredients hiding inside each other?"

The children may wonder how the butter has disappeared: "What has happened to the ingredients?" "Why do you think we need to add...?" "What do you think would happen if we left out...?"

Older children can be encouraged to describe what the changing ingredients look like.

Discuss with the children about the shapes of biscuits they wish to make, how many biscuits do they think they will make with their piece of biscuit dough? Could they make one large biscuit?

Learning about vegetables and fruit

With the importance of eating plenty of vegetables and fruit in our diets, we can stimulate interest in these foods with the children by encouraging them to try a variety of fruit and vegetables. Investing time in exploring and looking at a variety of fresh fruit and vegetables can help to establish healthy habits.

This activity is best suited to children aged over two years and conducted in small groups of up to ten children. It may lead into a tasting experience so ensure you inform parents prior to conducting the activity. You want the children to be able to see, feel and smell the fruit and vegetables.

You could choose to just focus on fruit or just on vegetables or both. Some children will be familiar with a variety of fruit and vegetables and others will not, so make sure your choice includes some more familiar and some less familiar items. This may also give an opportunity for children to try certain fruits and vegetables that they have never tasted before, or maybe they can be encouraged to try some they perceive they dislike.

If you are anticipating that the activity will include tasting then you will only be able to use fruit and vegetables that can be eaten raw. Try to choose from what is in season. Anything goes really, but some that work well are mushrooms, peppers, avocado, cucumber, tomato, apple, banana, orange, star fruit, Sharon fruit, strawberries, plums, potato, sweet potato, courgette and carrots.

An opportunity to learn about vegetables and fruit

The children will be able to see the whole fruit or vegetable and then, as it is cut, they can see how the shape changes and try to identify the parts. They can compare the size of the seeds and stones, e.g. an avocado stone, a pip from an orange and a seed from an apple core and then compare those with the cluster of seeds inside a pepper. How does the shape of a mushroom change once it is cut in half?

Look at the appearance of the knobbly sweet potato, a smooth butternut squash and a hairy kiwi fruit. The children will need to hold and feel all the fruit and vegetables to appreciate the contrasts. Thinking about smell, do any of the fruit and vegetables smell before they are cut, peeled or sliced or is it only after this has happened that you can smell them?

Before the children taste any of the fruit and vegetables, ask them which ones they have tasted before at home. Do they recognise them in the state in which you are showing them? Which would they like to taste? With some of the softer fruit and vegetables the older children could use round ended non-serrated table knives to cut or slice the fruit and vegetables, supporting their manipulative skills and ability to use different tools.

What do you need to do beforehand?

- Decide if you are going to use a mixture of fruit and vegetables or focus on one or the other. Decide how many different pieces there will be, will they all be able to eaten raw or will there be some just for show and not to be eaten?
- Consider the best way to lead the activity and what the level of involvement the children will have in terms of preparing the fruit and vegetables.
- Think about their responses and reactions. Will be recorded, will you use photographs and make notes about what they tried and what they liked. Making these notes can be useful for sharing with parents to help promote the healthy eating message. The parents may discover that their child likes something that they hadn't considered.

Responding to children's and babies' interests

What was popular? What did the children enjoy tasting the most? Could these particular fruit and vegetables be used in other ways to make salads or drinks or introduced to the snack time menu? Would it be possible to grow some of them in the setting garden? Could some of the seeds and/or pips be taken from some of the fruit and vegetables and planted, to see what the results might be. While they may not all grow, there will definitely be some degree of success. You might not be able to grow them in the garden, but you can put carrot, parsnip and turnip tops on a plate with a little water and they will grow green and hairy tops, which is fun for the children to experience.

Can the activity be repeated with other fruit and vegetables to extend the range the children have sampled? If they particularly liked mushrooms could you find different types for the children to see or could you look at citrus fruits, e.g. orange, grapefruit, blood orange, pink grapefruit, lemon and lime or perhaps a variety of fruit and vegetables all of one colour, e.g. red or yellow?

Potatoes and sweet potatoes could be boiled, and once cooled a little the children could mash them and compare the change of state with the raw vegetables. The mashing action is great for developing upper arm strength, through the lifting and pressing down motion.

Could they use a selection of the fruit and vegetables to create patterns or pictures by placing them in certain positions? The fruit and vegetables could also be sorted to variety of different criteria, e.g. colour, shape, size, with a stone inside, without a stone inside.

What worked well? Were there any fruit and vegetables that the children really didn't like? Why might this have been, would you introduce them again? Were there any children who were reluctant to taste anything? What was the children's understanding and knowledge about the importance of fruit and vegetables in our diet? How could this awareness and understanding be extended or introduced further depending on knowledge base? Did they enjoy the tasting or did they prefer other aspects of the activity?

Listening to children and talking with them

You could begin by asking the children what is on the table. Can they classify fruit and vegetables separately or do they see them differently? The very youngest children can be encouraged to handle them. The older twos and over threes may be able to describe what they feel like, rough, smooth, soft, hard, squidgy, knobbly. Can they smell anything? What are the differences between fruit and vegetables? Discuss the change of shape as they are cut or peeled and point out the different components e.g. peel, skin, core, seed, pips, flesh.

What do they think the produce will smell or taste like? Will it taste sweet or sour? After they have tasted some, encourage them to think about whether something was chewy, soft or crunchy. Which of the fruit and vegetables are they familiar with, which have they eaten before?

The questions you ask will be precipitated by the children's interests and their comments and questions, but some could be: "What do you think is the difference between fruit and vegetables?" "Which do you like?" "Which do you eat at home?" "What does the peel or the skin do and why is it important?" "What would happen if we planted the seeds?" "Do you think we can eat the seeds?" "Why do you think we need to cook this before we eat it?" "Where do we get fruit and vegetables from?"

Let the children lead the conversation.

Learning about how vegetables and fruit grow

To really appreciate food, children need to begin to find out where food comes from and understand that it doesn't just arrive pre-packaged at the supermarket. A visit to a pick your own farm or an allotment gives children a greater awareness of food, how it is grown and where it comes from.

Many pick your own farms have both fruit and vegetables and welcome visits from children. If you don't have a pick your own farm locally, or it would be difficult to visit, why not try your local allotment group, who may be able to facilitate a visit. Any visit needs careful planning.

The children can see the produce growing in large quantities in fields and may be able to pick, pull up or try digging up. This will hopefully trigger an interest, there is something satisfying about sourcing food for yourself and then eating it. If follow-up visits are linked with other activities in this book, e.g. courgette cake (see page 12) the children get a real sense of where food comes from.

What do you need to do beforehand?

- A considerable amount of forward planning is needed to arrange this visit.
- You will need to do a pre-visit to check they are happy for you to go there with the children and to carry out a risk assessment.
- Consider how you will get there and organise the travel arrangements.
- Work out the ratios and supervision necessary, seek permission from the parents and see if any will be able to accompany you on the trip.
- Consider how much time you want to spend there and plan which produce you would like the children to see, pick and dig. Are they going to bring the produce back to the setting, will it then be eaten, cooked or taken home?
- If any children have specific food allergies or intolerances, particularly with strawberries, ensure all relevant adults know about this.
- Discuss with the children beforehand where you are going and what will happen and ask them what they think they will see, do and discover. Some children may assume they will see animals if they are going to a farm.
- Have a wet weather plan, consider appropriate clothing and whether you can still visit the farm or allotment.

An opportunity to learn about how vegetables and fruit grow

Children are outdoors engaging with a natural environment and making discoveries about food. They can see how produce grows near the ground, under the ground or on a bush. They can search for strawberries hiding under leaves, or raspberries near the bottom of a cane. They can be encouraged to think about how they know when a fruit is ripe, the difference between a green strawberry and a vibrant red one.

If the farm grows vegetables they can see the plant that grows above ground with the vegetable below. You may see the actual vegetable poking through the ground, e.g. carrots and onions. Could they pull that vegetable up or does it need to be dug up? If you take small forks and trowels with you, the children may be able to dig up the vegetables.

This is an opportunity to help children understand why fruit and vegetables are important in our diet, to feed our bodies and help us to grow and be strong.

Responding to children's and babies' interests

There will need to be a certain amount of planning. You want to allow for some spontaneity during the visit, although some responses to the interests will need to be back at the setting. Babies may simply observe and handle the fruit and vegetables, sitting on the ground in the field, seeing, smelling and hearing what is around them. Toddlers can help pick strawberries and carry their own punnet.

Do the children enjoy picking the fruit or do they prefer walking around, looking at everything? Older children could use a digital camera to take photos of fruit or vegetables, if they are reluctant to pick fruit or dig the vegetables.

If they are excited by a particularly large, small or odd-shaped fruit or vegetable, talk about how it compares with others, do they think it will taste the same or will it be different? They could take a photo recording their finds.

The children will undoubtedly want to taste the produce, which could happen as a picnic at the farm with the ready to eat produce. A second tasting session can take place in the setting with vegetables that need to be washed and/or cooked prior to eating. This links in with the vegetable and fruit tasting activity (see page 20).

If they enjoy digging, you can extend digging opportunities in the setting, both in terms of an area to dig and tools to use, maybe burying items for them to dig up.

Once back in the setting the children will want to talk about the trip. Use the photos to make a memory book with the children's thoughts and observations.

Perhaps you could extend children's interest with a visit to a supermarket, green grocers or a garden centre to look at younger plants and seeds. If you go to a garden centre make sure you plan the visit carefully beforehand.

Time for you to think

Was the trip successful? What aspects did the children enjoy the most? Did the timings for the trip and plan for the visit work well or would you make changes if you were to repeat the visit. Could you grow some of your own produce in the setting garden? What surprises did you get about the children's engagement or perhaps reluctance to participate? Did you observe any skills in action you didn't know the children had or did they display knowledge through chat and discussion that you were unaware they had?

Listening to children and talking with them

Being somewhere completely different out of doors is bound to lead to conversation and questions from the children. Encourage them to describe what they can see and smell. Can they describe the fruit and vegetables they see? Which can they name and recognise as you wander round. Don't overload the children – you want them to enjoy and absorb the experience; taking in everything for themselves and process their own thoughts and observations. This needs to be sensitively supported with input from you.

Ask the children why they think some vegetables grow under the ground and some above the ground – what difference do they think it makes? How do they think they can find and dig up the vegetables hiding under the ground? See what they can name and describe, and what you need to help them with.

When looking at the soft fruit, how do they know which fruits are ripe and ready to eat? What do they think makes them ripe and ready to eat? Ensure your questions encourage reflective thought and problem solving. "How long do you think it has taken to grow all these fruit and vegetables?" "Would the children like to pick and eat them?"

If the children are particularly interested in certain fruits or vegetables, encourage further thought about those, e.g. "Can you see that the strawberry plants are surrounded by a straw bed, do you think that is why they are called strawberries?"

Learning about a drinks factory

I've called this activity the 'drinks factory' because I observed a group of children playing in the water tray, where the water was coloured purple. In their imaginative play they had a Ribena factory using lots of tubes, piping and containers. This led to the idea of an adult-led activity mixing drinks called 'the drinks factory'.

This is an adult-led activity, but has a lot of freedom for the children to experiment and make decisions for themselves. Provide the children with a selection of fruit juices, water, sparkling water and fruit. They choose what they want to combine to make their own fruit cocktail. You can add to the fun by providing bendy or curly straws, or cocktail umbrellas (but make sure you cut the points off).

The children can see how the colours combine and change as they mix their drink. Each ingredient needs to be available in a jug or from an easy-pour carton, so that the children can take as much control as possible. This activity is suitable for twos or over, although less able children may need help to access the activity.

You could also create smoothies using fruit, milk or yoghurt. They could be mixed in a blender, so children can see the ingredients whizzing and changing, or they could use a hand blender to do it themselves.

What do you need to do beforehand?

- Collect together the drinks ingredients, jugs for pouring, plastic glasses, straws and any other accessories. Encourage the children to help with this process.
- Talk with the children about how you are going to set up the activity – they might suggest staging it indoors or outdoors in a 'café'.
- Select what juices and water are going to be available to the children, if you are going to set up to make smoothies or if you are going to provide a choice.
- Prepare pictures of the fruit used to make their juices or match with the real fruit so the children can make the connection and see what they are putting into their drink.
- If you are going to use a blender or an electric hand blender ensure that it has had an electrical safety check, and consider where it will be plugged in and how to manage the possible trailing flex. Think of the best way for the children to use it under close adult supervision.
- Freeze a selection of different shaped ice cubes for the children to add to their drinks, these could then be placed in an ice bucket with tongs, for the children to use.

An opportunity to learn about a drinks factory

This is a chance to explore different flavours, look at the colours of the juices and to make a choice for themselves, encouraging the children to try something new both in terms of an activity and a drink. There may also be an element of surprise with what the drink looks and tastes like. If you have provided the actual fruit they can compare the colour, appearance and flavour with the juice.

You could also have different-shaped ice cubes for the children to add to their drinks, so they can see them melting and listen to the sound they make as they hit the liquid.

The children will have a chance to pour the juice to make their drinks. How full should their glass be? Why is it important not to overfill the glass? Think about the glass being half full or half empty. What is the difference between drinking through a straw or from the glass – which do they prefer? What makes the juice move up the straw?

Responding to children's and babies' interests

This activity features various elements of choice and preferences, so you could make a record, perhaps a chart, showing what the children chose to put in their drinks, and what was the most popular ingredient. How many children chose that ingredient? Which was the least popular? Was there anything not chosen by the children? You could use photos to illustrate the chart and the children could record through a mark making activity what they chose for their drink, or what they liked and did not like.

If the ice cubes are popular you could freeze cubes with pieces of fruit in them to go into the drinks, or freeze the juice itself. Alternatively the children could make ice lollies using watered fruit juice or squash. To do this you will need wooden lolly sticks and moulds for the lollies.

What do the children think about the colours created by their drinks? You could introduce, for example, the use of grenadine which is a syrup usually made from pomegranates to colour the drinks, making a sunset effect.

You could set up a drinks factory in the water tray with empty plastic bottles and juice containers, tubing or piping, and plastic glasses so that they can explore imaginatively. The children could choose what colour they would like the water to be, so that it represents a particular drink.

You could set up a role play experience of a café or drinks stall for the children to enjoy, perhaps incorporating the water play.

Was a good range of choices available for the children that they liked to make their drinks? Were there any surprises in the children's knowledge matching the actual fruit to the drink? Could the experience have been presented differently, were they able to manipulate the jugs and cartons so they could pour their drinks themselves? What questions did the children ask? Did they demonstrate an interest in what other children had made, did they want to try each other's drinks?

Listening to children and talking with them

Chat to the children about what drinks they like. What drinks do they enjoy at the setting and at home? Do they just have water? What do they think makes a good drink, something with bubbles or in a special carton? Do they have their drink using a straw? Ask them: "If you have a drink with bubbles, do you sometimes feel like they have got into your nose and make it tickle?"

Study the fruit juice cartons, what sort of juice do they think is in each carton? How do they think the juice was taken out of the fruit? What do they think happened to the apple peel and the apple core, is it in the juice?

If they chose to put ice into their own drink ask them to listen carefully to what they can hear, wait for their responses and ideas. Can they hear the ice crackle as it drops into the liquid and the sound of the cubes knocking against each other? What do they think will happen to the ice cubes? How will the ice change their drink? Will it just be the temperature that changes or will it change in other ways?

Give simple statement instructions to help the children mix and pour their drinks. It is important to use positive statements which help the children understand what to do rather than what not to do, for example; "Put one hand on the handle of the jug and one on the front" "Put a hand on either side of the carton as you pour" "Hold the jug a little way above the glass so it is easy to pour."

Learning about play dough

Play dough is fun and versatile, and there is so much we can do to make it more exciting and enhance the children's experience. Dough can be used to introduce children to skills associated with cooking. Part of the attraction of dough is that it can be used by all children across a wide age range. They can be

What do you need to do beforehand?

- Decide which recipe to make, ensuring you have the ingredients. Decide what added ingredients you are going to experiment with and how many types of dough you and the children are going to make.
- Will the dough be presented on a table top or perhaps in a tuff spot or even directly on the floor.
- Will you be providing tools, e.g. cutters, rolling pins, scissors, baking trays or will the children simply be using their hands. You could make the tools available nearby so the children have a choice.
- Will you be all making the dough in one large bowl or will the children be making their own in smaller bowls, with small cups to measure with. If the children are making their own dough, are you going to provide a choice in terms of added ingredients or will they be making a basic dough? If you do this activity several times you can introduce different variations to those children who know what they are doing.
- Remember that for this activity contact allergies must be planned for as well.
- Consider the level of supervision, will the adult be there just when the children are making the dough in case any support is required. Will the adult move away from the activity or will the adult be guided by the children's response as to whether to stay or not? For example younger children will need more careful supervision.

Recipe for play dough – option one

2 cups of flour, 2 cups of salt, splash of oil, water as necessary. This dough has a shiny gleam, cuts easily and will store well in an airtight container.

Recipe for play dough – option two

2 cups of flour, water as necessary. This is a great dough for when you run out of salt, but it won't keep.

Recipe for play dough – option three

2 cups of flour, 2 cups of salt, water as necessary. This is a salt dough recipe and will dry hard after about 40 minutes in a low temperature oven. This dough will store in an airtight container.

involved in making dough using simple recipes. Our recipes all work well and are easy for them to make.

When presenting dough to the children, don't always put out tools, let them explore the dough with their hands.

An opportunity to learn about play dough

Play dough supports many aspects of development, particularly physical manipulating using a variety of different skills: prodding, poking, squeezing and kneading, building strength in the fingers and hands and supporting muscle control particularly in the upper arm.

Counting and mathematical understanding of quantity as well as hand and eye co-ordination are supported and made more challenging through the making of dough, particularly if the children are following a pictorial recipe card.

Scientific observations are made, as the children mix the dough and observe the change of state as the dry ingredients combine with the water. They can experience the different properties and textures of the dough when making the different recipes.

Variety is important, so children experience different textures, densities and smells. As well as varying the recipe, you should experiment with different flours and added ingredients. One cup of one of the following can be used in any of these recipes to replace one cup of plain flour: self-raising flour, wholemeal, gram, rice, pasta, potato starch, corn meal or ground rice.

Use bubble bath in dough instead of water, experiment with added ingredients: angel delight, jelly crystals, coloured rice, mustard, blancmange, toothpaste or custard powder.

If you put raisins into a glass of lemonade they will bob up and down on the bubbles. This will fascinate the children, and can then be used to make a soft dough.

Responding to children's and babies' interests

For babies and the youngest children build up the density and texture of the dough they use, so it gradually becomes harder and with a rougher texture.

The children may have ideas as to what ingredients they would like to add to the dough.

They may also wish to use the play dough with other experiences – transport it for a role play of a picnic or take into the home corner.

Time for you to think

What did you discover about the children's enjoyment of the dough? How did they engage with it, and how was it used? What dough did they like or not like, what added ingredients did they find particularly fascinating? What other ideas has this generated? Did they use the dough in an unusual way? Could the experience be enhanced or developed or better presented next time? Could independence be encouraged for older children where the basic ingredients are just on the shelf, so they can get them out when they want and make up some dough?

Listening to children and talking with them

Children like to chat while playing with dough. Often this conversation is nothing to do with the actual play dough experience, but something unrelated, still what they say is of interest to the adult listener. Enjoy this chatter and don't always try to find in it a potential new learning experience, just use it as an opportunity to find out more about the children.

With babies and young children in the pre-linguistic or the very early linguistic stage you can engage in parallel talk, where you describe what the child is doing, to give words to their actions and reactions.

Think about your questions and listen carefully to what the children say, trying not to interrupt them: "What do we need to do to make the dough less sticky?" "What is happening as you add ...?" "Is that a heavy dough or a light dough, do they feel the same?" (This depends on the ingredients used to make the dough.) "What does that smell make you think of?" "Can you hide your hands in the dough?" "Can you make the dough stretch across the table?"

Children will often ask the adult to make something out of the dough, e.g. a cat. It is important to respond, inviting the child to make one themselves to show you how to make the cat.

Allow time for any responses and for the conversation to develop.

Learning about icing and icing bags

Icing bags may be used for children to ice their own biscuits, but are also perfect for little hands to grab and use instead of a paintbrush or other mark making tool. As they are soft and squidgy, they fit the hand perfectly. They can be filled with paint for use on paper, or filled with icing for decorating a biscuit or using on card (paper tends to be too porous for the icing).

You can use either disposable icing bags or plastic reusable bags. Children often prefer to use them without a nozzle, as it can be easier for them to squeeze the paint or icing through. Some reusable icing bags have a large hole at the tip, in which case a nozzle would need to be used. Once the children have developed their skills, nozzles of different shapes and sizes can be used.

This activity is very accessible and is suitable for children aged two and above. Depending on their dexterity, you can simply adjust the size and height of the icing bag.

An opportunity to learn about icing and icing bags

This provides an interesting mark making experience as the children swirl the icing or paint over the card or paper. It is an opportunity to make a permanent mark, whether that is a pattern or something more definite. For some children, this will be an unexpected discovery, depending on their stage of development and their prior experience.

While it requires a combination of quite complex skills, it is a relatively easy activity for all children to access through trial and error. They have to understand the need to apply slight pressure to squeeze the paint or icing out of the bag, how to hold the icing bag upright, and the need to hold the bag at a height above the surface. They will discover that holding it at different heights produces varied results.

These techniques support hand and eye co-ordination, manipulative skills and use of tools for mark making, while encouraging creativity as they make patterns and representations. Some children may explore further by putting their hands into their creations, adding a further sensory dimension to the experience.

Responding to children's and babies' interests

If the children are interested in colour mixing or creating multi-coloured patterns, try putting two colours

What do you need to do beforehand?

- Prepare the icing bags so they are an appropriate size for the children to use and decide if you are going to use nozzles, or simply carefully cut the tips. If you use nozzles provide a selection so the children can choose for themselves.
- If you are using disposable icing bags ensure they are tough plastic with an easy grip, so that they will not slip and slide in the children's hands.
- Collect together the icing sugar, water and food colouring so you can make up the icing with the children and they can decide on what colours they would like the icing to be.
- If you are using paint, provide a selection of ready mix paint colours or mix powder paint colours with the children. Experiment first to ensure you get the right consistency to pipe with (so that it won't flow too fast out of the bag or be so thick that it is impossible to manipulate).
- Let the children decide if they are going to make permanent creations on card or paper, or if they are going to experiment using the bags directly on a table top or tray.

into the icing bag at the same time. Do they keep separate or do they combine? What would happen if you mixed icing and paint, how would that change the appearance and consistency?

Provide decorations to sprinkle onto their creations, this could be hundreds and thousands, sugar strands or sequins. If you have used white icing, give the children pipettes of food colouring, to blob onto the icing – the food colouring will stay on the icing and not spill over, clinging to its position. This could be extended by using a blunt pencil or similar to drag the food colouring across the icing thus creating a pattern.

Encourage experimentation with the use of different shaped nozzles and different consistencies of paint and icing, and involve the children in mixing these. You may need to use butter icing to squeeze through larger nozzles, mixing the icing sugar with margarine so it holds its shape.

Could you make a giant icing bag and fill with damp sand, and ice into the tuff spot or sand tray? Can you make one big enough for more than one child to use at the same time? Polythene would be a good material to use for this purpose and you could use a large yoghurt pot as a nozzle.

For a further extension try making icing sugar pictures, brushing a watery solution of icing sugar and water (about 2 tablespoons of icing sugar and 150ml of water) liberally over card and then sprinkle over with powder paint. The powder paint will disperse in the liquid solution, creating a pattern. Encourage the children to explore different ways to use and manipulate the icing bags when making shapes or patterns. This will give further opportunities for them to express their creativity.

Time for you to think

Did the children enjoy the activity? Was it easy for them to manipulate and use the icing bags, had they been cut to the right size? Did any of the children struggle to squeeze the icing out and use the right amount of pressure? Was it better to use nozzles in the bags or to simply cut the tip of the icing bag? What did you discover about the children's mark making skills and understanding of mark making, what did they choose to represent? Did they create patterns? How did they use the colours? Was it more effective to use paint or to use icing?

Listening to children and talking with them

As you are making the icing ask the children how you could make it thicker or runnier. What do they think will be best to use in the bags? Ask them about where they have seen icing and what it was like. You could look at pictures of iced biscuits, cakes and cupcakes to see the different designs and types of icing.

Be ready for questions and comments from the children, such as: "What will happen if I move my arms really fast as I ice?" "What if I hold the bag up higher?" Think about simple instructions you can give to the children to help them manipulate and use the icing bag, while modelling yourself. "Hold the bag straight so the top is pointing to the ceiling, with both of your hands round the bag" or "Squeeze the bag very gently so the icing can escape from the bottom" "Can you move your arms around a little bit, so the bag moves over the card, and you can make the icing draw a pattern?"

This activity requires concentration, so the children will need to be quiet to focus on what they are doing. They may make comments about what they are doing or about the patterns and marks the icing has created on the card. If you sense they are absorbed don't interrupt with questions. Make statements about what they are doing: "The icing looks like a snail trail" "The icing looks like it is flying through the air as it drops from the icing bag onto the card." Wait and see how the children react.

Learning about experimental cooking

This activity is about freedom to explore and experiment with a variety of ingredients. There is no right or wrong way of doing this – it is about learning through the process and the suggestion of endless possibilities. The children are given different ingredients, both wet and dry, solid and liquid in containers, and left to combine them. These could be placed directly on a table top or in a tuff spot for the youngest children. They then use their hands to explore and combine, relishing the sensory experience. As some practitioners may feel that food should be 'eaten' rather than 'wasted' with children's explorations, or thrown away after they have experimented with it, it is important to be aware of the learning opportunities that playing with food gives to them.

For the older children, the mixing could be done in bowls using a range of tools. Leave a selection of them, e.g. wooden spoon, metal spoon, rotary whisk, available so the children can choose a tool if they wish. They could have access to weighing scales for imitative play and you could also allow use of a hand blender under adult supervision.

Often, with this type of activity, practitioners unnecessarily worry about the youngest children putting the food in their mouths. Provided you have done an allergy check, none of these ingredients will harm the children. Putting items in their mouths is part of the process of sensory exploration and with careful and sensitive supervision this should not be a problem.

What do you need to do beforehand?

- Make your choice of ingredients, perhaps from what is in the cupboard as the random nature of the selection can bring about more interesting results. Ensure you have a good variety with wet and dry ingredients. These ingredients could include flour, salt, rice, ground rice, margarine, water, jelly, tomato puree, tea, coffee, herbs, spices, corn meal, potato starch and sugar.
- Decide how the activity will be presented to the children, this is particularly relevant for the two year olds and under: high chair tray, table top or tuff spot.
- Select any tools you wish to make available for the older children e.g. rotary whisk, balloon whisk.
- Make sure you are aware how anything unsafe will be managed, e.g. a hand blender.
- Will the children be encouraged to work alone or together as a small group?
- The adult will need to stand back from the activity to allow for complete freedom, but consider any necessary supervision.

An opportunity to learn about experimental cooking

The children will be pouring, squeezing, scooping, smearing and mixing the ingredients, combining them together and finding out about their properties. Is the mixture smooth, runny, lumpy or thick? Can this state be changed? They are creating and seeing the reactions of combined ingredients, the change of state and cause and effect, while making connections about these concepts.

Let children have complete freedom, encouraging curiosity and exploration. This will hopefully bring about a 'what would happen if...?' thought process. Creativity is ignited and the use of imagination stimulates the desire to explore.

For the younger children, muscle strength in the hands and upper arms is stimulated through mixing and manipulating the ingredients. The older children can refine skills like gripping with their hands through the use of tools which are controlled in different ways. A rotary whisk is an excellent example, as it has to be held steady with one hand, and the handle turned with the other hand.

Responding to children's and babies' interests

Take your clues from what the children are doing, add tools if requested or if you think they will enhance the experience. This might include weighing scales or different types of whisks, containers, sieves, strainers, mashers, cutters, paper cake cases and spoons. With support from the adult, older children could use a milk frother. The children may like to bake their concoctions in the oven, to see what the finished results looks like, if not necessarily to taste. As this is a very free experience, you need to respond in the spur of the moment.

An adult-supported activity could follow, where the children make up their own recipes from a selection of ingredients thinking about what might work well together. This could include experience with herbs and spices, smelling and feeling them either fresh or from a jar. What happens when they rub or crush the fresh herbs, can they tear the leaves? The recipes could then be tried out. This encourages a creative and inquisitive approach to cooking and feeds into children's natural curiosity.

For the under-twos, consider what aspects of the tactile experience they have enjoyed. Was it dry lumpy ingredients, dry fine ingredients or wet ingredients? Can you add something completely contrasting in terms of texture, properties and appearance e.g. ice cubes, pasta shapes?

Be creative. Food and cooking lends itself to a variety of experiences, that all children will be able to enjoy with the appropriate supervision and support.

Time for you to think

Were you surprised by the children's engagement? How long did they spend absorbed in the experience? Did they enjoy using their hands or did they prefer using tools? Consider what you learnt about the value of the experience, in that there was no end product. Were the children happy to simply explore with no specific end result? Did they like to simply feel or did they prefer to combine the ingredients? Where could you move on next time, providing the experience on a larger scale, perhaps in a tuff spot or narrowing down what ingredients are provided for the children.

Listening to children and talking with them

Adult talk needs to be minimal, especially with the youngest children, so they are allowed to be completely absorbed in the experience. You need to stand back and let them engage and observe their verbal and non-verbal communication, what they are enjoying, and their facial expressions displaying reactions to the tactile experience.

You may engage in some parallel talk, where, on occasions, you may use descriptive vocabulary to describe the sound and feel of the ingredients or ask questions like: "Does that feel squidgy?" "I wonder what would happen if you added some more?" "I wonder what would happen if you added some water?"

With older children try to use affirmative statements, or wait until they choose to engage you in conversation or ask for your comment. With this type of deeply absorbing activity, questions can be intrusive, so construct and use them carefully, e.g. "What could you add to make the ingredients easier to move around the bowl?" "Can you whisk it very fast or do you think it would be better to use the whisk slowly?" Follow up on what the children are doing, e.g. if one is whisking very fast say "Look how the ingredients are bubbling and going frothy as you whisk" "It is all squelching through the masher like worms" "What do you think that would taste like if you were to eat it?"

"Can you eat some foods both raw and cooked?"

Reflections on learning about food and cooking

Consider overall how the babies and children have gained experience and knowledge, learnt and developed through these activities. How has development been stimulated, what skills and techniques have been learnt? How has their awareness of food and cooking increased?

Were you surprised at what the children enjoyed and the extent of their knowledge and understanding? How did you make these discoveries about the learning, was it through observation, or what the children communicated either verbally or non-verbally to you? How do you feel you can move forward and extend their interest?

Will your approach to planned activities for cooking change in any way? Do you feel that your confidence with these activities has increased? Are there any activities or experiences that you will revisit and approach from a different angle? Could cooking become a more regular feature in the routine of your setting? How can this be further supported through imaginary play experiences?

Are there individual children who have displayed a specific interest or skill? Can you explore a variety of cookery books with the children, are there any more visits you could organise to develop their interest?

Finding out more

- Baxter, N. and Stevenson, P. (1994) *The Enormous Turnip*, Ladybird.

- Bennett, J. (2006) *Tasty Poems*, OUP.

- French, V. (1998) *Oliver's Fruit Salad*, Hodder.

- *Healthy Eating*, (2007) Practical Pre-School Books.

- Kidd, S. and Musters, F. (2004) *Cook and Learn Together*, Practical Pre-School Books.

- Sparks Linfield, R. (2008) *Planning for Learning Through Farms*, Practical Pre-School Books.

- Sparks Linfield, R. (2008) *Planning for Learning Through Food*, Practical Pre-School Books.

- Vernon Lloyd, J. & Burrows, J. (2010) *The Giant Jam Sandwich*, Red Fox.

- www.nhs.uk/Change4Life

England: Statutory Framework for the Early Years Foundation Stage (2012): www.foundationyears.org.uk/early-years-foundation-stage-2012/

Northern Ireland: CCEA (2011) 'Curricular Guidance for Pre-school Education': www.rewardinglearning.org.uk/curriculum/pre_school/index.asp; CCEA (2006) 'Understanding the Foundation Stage': www.nicurriculum.org.uk/docs/foundation_stage/UF_web.pdf

Scotland: Learning and Teaching Scotland (2010) 'Pre-birth to Three: Positive Outcomes for Scotland's Children and Families': www.ltscotland.org.uk/earlyyears/; The Scottish Government (2008) 'Curriculum for Excellence: Building the Curriculum 3: A Framework for Learning and Teaching'.

Wales: Welsh Assembly (2008) 'Framework for Children's Learning for 3 to 7-year-olds in Wales': http://wales.gov.uk/topics/educationandskills/schoolshome/curriculuminwales/arevisedcurriculumforwales/foundationphase/?lang=en